EARTH & SPACE

Let's Investigate

by Ruth Owen and Victoria Dobney

Consultant:

Nicky Waller

Ruby Tuesday Books

Published in 2019 by Ruby Tuesday Books Ltd.

Copyright © 2019 Ruby Tuesday Books Ltd.

All rights reserved. No part of this publication may be reproduced in whole or in part, stored in any retrieval system, or transmitted in any form or by any means, electronic, mechanical, photocopying, recording, or otherwise, without written permission from the publisher.

Editor: Mark J. Sachner
Designer: Emma Randall
Production: John Lingham

Photo credits:

Alamy: 25 (bottom left); ESA: 22 (bottom right), 23 (top right); Getty Images: 15; NASA: 4, 5 (bottom), 11, 17 (top), 21 (top), 22 (top right), 23 (bottom left), 24 (top right), 26, 29 (top); Ruby Tuesday Books: 17 (top), 18—19, 20, 25 (top), 27 (bottom), 28 (top); Science Photo Library: 6—7, 28 (bottom); Shutterstock: Cover, 1, 5 (top), 8—9, 10, 12—13, 14, 16, 21 (bottom), 22 (top left), 22 (bottom left), 23 (top left), 23 (bottom right), 24 (top left), 24 (bottom left), 25 (bottom right); Superstock: 24 (bottom right), 27 (top).

ISBN 978-1-78856-036-8

Printed in China by Toppan Leefung Printing Limited

www.rubytuesdaybooks.com

Contents

The download button shows there are free
worksheets or other resources available.
Go to:
www.rubytuesdaybooks.com/scienceKS2

Our Very Special Planet

Imagine you are an astronaut heading into space. The countdown is finally over. A deafening roar bursts from the base of the rocket that is launching your spacecraft up into the sky.

Finally, you leave Earth's **atmosphere**. From the window you can now see the blackness of space and a beautiful bright blue, green and brown world.

It's **planet** Earth — our home in the **universe**.

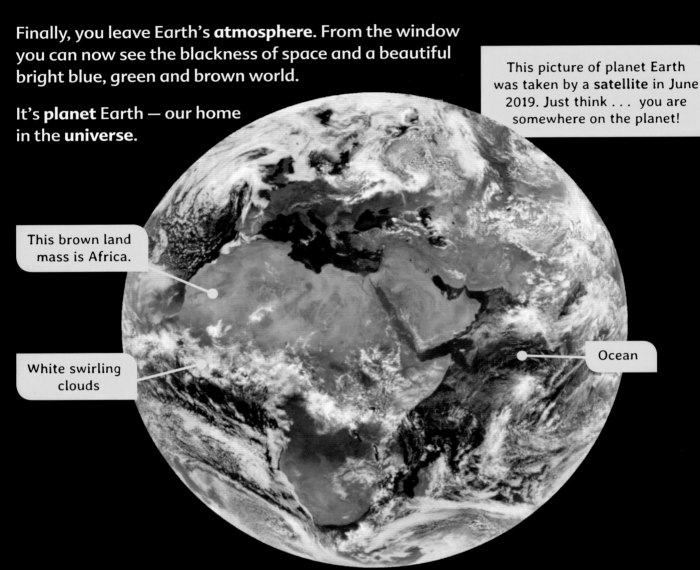

This picture of planet Earth was taken by a **satellite** in June 2019. Just think . . . you are somewhere on the planet!

This brown land mass is Africa.

Ocean

White swirling clouds

Scientists estimate there are more than 8.7 million different kinds of living things on Earth.

Our Blue Planet

You've probably heard Earth being called "The Blue Planet". That's because about three-quarters of its surface is covered by water and from space, Earth looks blue. Earth's oceans are thousands of kilometres wide and in places they are more than 6 km deep.

Inside Planet Earth

Earth is made up of three layers called the **crust**, the **mantle** and the **core**.

Thick Crust

Where there is land, Earth's crust is 24 to 56 kilometres thick.

Beneath the oceans it is 5 to 8 km thick.

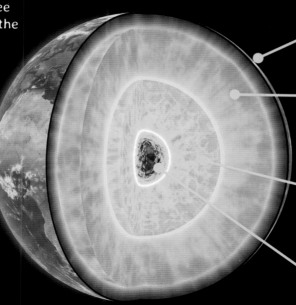

Crust
Earth's crust is made of many different kinds of rock.

Mantle
Here it is so hot that the rock becomes soft like toffee.

Outer Core
The outer layer of the core is made of molten iron and nickel. Here, temperatures reach about 4400°C.

Inner Core
The inner core is a solid mass of metal that's about 6000°C. That's hotter than the Sun's surface.

Mind-Boggling Space Stuff

Our Earth is just a tiny, tiny part of a universe that is so vast even numbers such as billions and trillions aren't big enough to measure it! When scientists study space, they have to think BIG. They use their imaginations, ask lots of questions, develop **theories** and go looking for **evidence** to try to explain what's out there and how all that space stuff got here!

Let's Talk!

It's your turn to think like a space scientist. Earth formed about 4.5 billion years ago. How do you think this happened?

(The answer is coming up later in this book.)

Earth's Atmosphere

Earth's atmosphere is a protective layer of **gases** that surrounds our planet. By day, it stops the Sun's light making the planet too hot. At night, because heat from the daytime is stored in the atmosphere, Earth stays warm even in the absence of sunlight.

Earth's atmosphere

The atmosphere reaches up to about 120 kilometres above Earth's surface.

The Beginning of Time

What do we mean when we say the beginning of time? About 13.7 billion years ago, there was nothing. No Earth, no **stars**, no space, no universe, no time — just nothing!

Then the universe was born. How?

Scientists cannot say for sure, but most scientists believe that it went something like this. In one trillion-trillion-trillionth of a second, a tiny **energy**-filled speck, thousands of times smaller than a pinhead, began to **expand**. This was the start of the universe.

The burning-hot fireball of a new universe grew and expanded. In less than a minute, it was billions of kilometres across and still growing. It kept on growing bigger and bigger, and scientists believe the universe is still expanding today.

This theory of how the universe began is called the big bang theory because the universe expanded incredibly quickly, like an explosion!

As the universe grew, it began to cool down. After a few hundred thousand years, the energy in the universe turned into **matter** and formed clouds of gases. These gas clouds contained all the ingredients for making stars, planets and everything else that we know.

Big Science Questions

If there was nothing before the big bang, where did the energy-filled speck come from? That's a huge question that scientists are trying to answer. A scientist who studies the universe and how it began is a **cosmologist**. This type of science is called cosmology.

Our Expanding Universe

What do we mean when we say the universe is still expanding today?
Imagine your playground is the universe. You start
running towards the fence that surrounds the playground.
But the playground keeps on expanding at high speed. Even if you could
run as fast as a rocket, you could still never touch the fence because the
playground is always growing bigger and bigger in every direction.

As stars were
born, they formed
into **galaxies**. A galaxy is
an enormous collection of
stars, dust and gases that is
moving through space.
A single galaxy may be
made up of millions or
even trillions
of stars.

Galaxy

Making Planet Earth

The universe came into being about 13.7 billion years ago. So when did our Earth form and how did it happen?

To answer this question, many scientists have studied the stars and outer space and this is their theory.

Billions of years ago, a beautiful cloud of dust and gas called a **nebula** was floating in the universe. This cloud contained the ingredients to make stars, planets and even you!

About 4.5 billion years ago, some of the gas and dust in the cloud began to collect together. It became a massive spinning sphere, or ball. As the sphere spun around, a disc of gases and dust formed around the sphere.

Star Factories

A nebula is a cloud of gas and dust trillions of kilometres wide. The word *nebula* is the Latin word for "cloud". Nebulae are often called star factories because they are the places in space where stars form, or are born.

Super-hot sphere

Disc of dust and gases

As the disc grew larger, all that matter pressed in on the sphere. Pressure and heat began to build up. The sphere's core reached temperatures of 10 million degrees Celsius.

Finally, the sphere got so hot, it **ignited** and became a star. That star is our Sun. The leftover gas and dust continued to spin in a vast disc around the Sun.

The Sun

Planets and rocks spinning around the newly formed star

Over time, the matter in the disc began to clump together. It formed eight large planets, including our Earth. It also formed smaller planets called **dwarf planets**, as well as **moons, comets** and rocky **asteroids**. All these objects continued to travel around and around the Sun and they still do today.

Together, the Sun and all the objects that orbit it are known as the solar system.

A new planet forming

Mind-Boggling Space Stuff

You might think you're sitting perfectly still reading this book. But in fact you are zooming through space at about 30 kilometres per second! You, your school, your home and everything else on Earth is constantly moving around the Sun at high speed.

Let's Talk!

Our Earth is one of eight planets in the solar system. What are the names of the other seven?
(You will find out the answer later in the book.)

Our Star, the Sun

The Sun is a star — one of the trillions of stars in the universe. It looks huge in the sky, but that's just because it is nearer to Earth than all the other stars we see at night.

Like all stars, the Sun is a giant ball of gases that produce heat and light. Without the Sun's energy, Earth would just be a dark, frozen lump of rock.

Earth is about 150 million kilometres from the Sun. This distance is very important for our planet. If we were any closer, it would be so hot all the water on Earth would dry up. If Earth were any further from the Sun, it would be so cold all the water would freeze.

Having just the right temperatures on Earth means there is liquid water here which is essential for the survival of animals, plants and other living things.

⚠ WARNING

You should NEVER look directly at the Sun because it will badly damage your eyes – even if you are wearing sunglasses. Your eyes would act a little like a magnifying glass. They would focus the Sun's powerful, bright light into your eyes and burn them!

Super Speedy Sunlight

Light is the fastest thing in the universe. It travels from the Sun towards Earth at 299,792 kilometres per second. If you could move that fast, you'd be able to whizz around Earth 7.5 times in just one second! Because Earth is so far from the Sun, however, it takes sunlight eight minutes to get here.

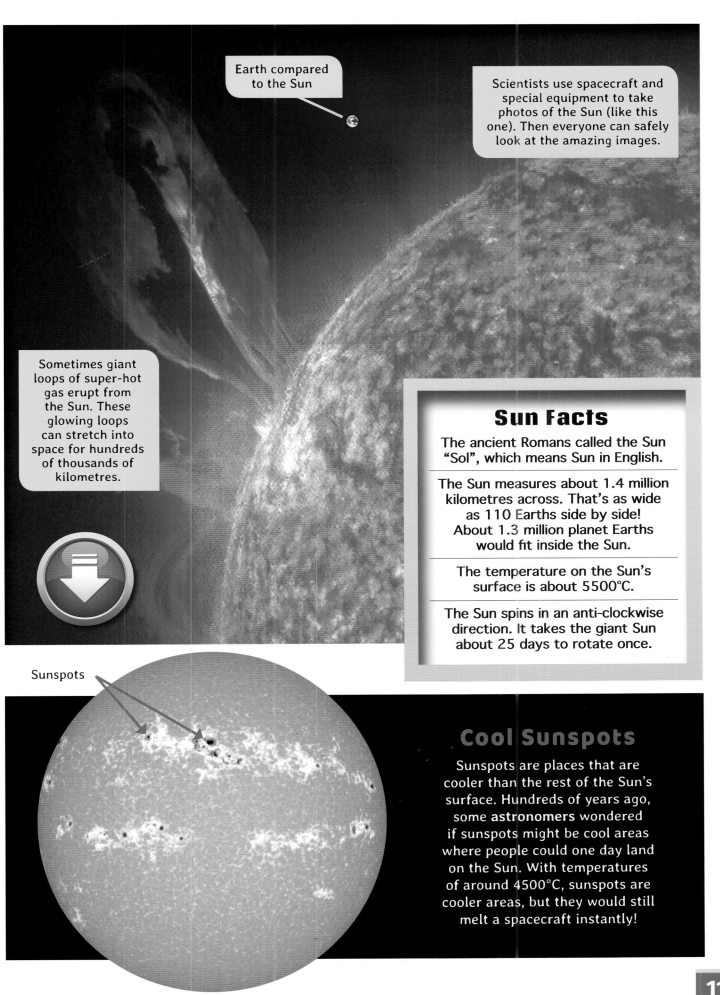

Earth compared to the Sun

Scientists use spacecraft and special equipment to take photos of the Sun (like this one). Then everyone can safely look at the amazing images.

Sometimes giant loops of super-hot gas erupt from the Sun. These glowing loops can stretch into space for hundreds of thousands of kilometres.

Sun Facts

The ancient Romans called the Sun "Sol", which means Sun in English.

The Sun measures about 1.4 million kilometres across. That's as wide as 110 Earths side by side! About 1.3 million planet Earths would fit inside the Sun.

The temperature on the Sun's surface is about 5500°C.

The Sun spins in an anti-clockwise direction. It takes the giant Sun about 25 days to rotate once.

Sunspots

Cool Sunspots

Sunspots are places that are cooler than the rest of the Sun's surface. Hundreds of years ago, some **astronomers** wondered if sunspots might be cool areas where people could one day land on the Sun. With temperatures of around 4500°C, sunspots are cooler areas, but they would still melt a spacecraft instantly!

Earth's Days and Years

As a planet orbits the Sun, it also rotates, or spins. It takes Earth 24 hours to rotate once.

The reason we have day and night in each 24-hour period is because Earth is spinning. When the place where you live faces towards the Sun, it is daytime for you. As Earth spins away from the Sun's light, darkness falls and it is night.

As Earth spins, it is slightly tilted to one side.

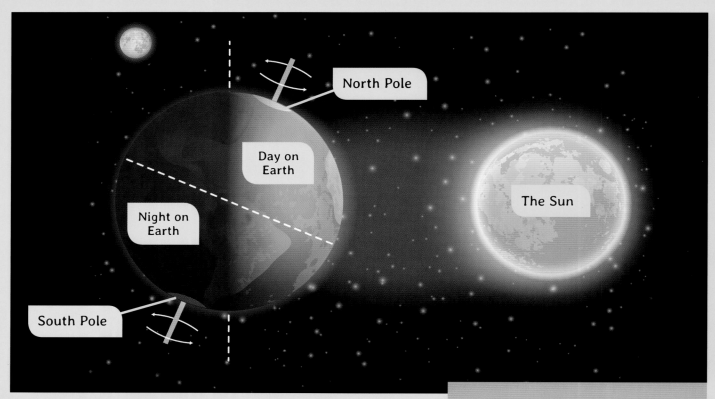

North Pole

Day on Earth

The Sun

Night on Earth

South Pole

The Sun's position in the sky during the summer

East

West

Mind-Boggling Space Stuff

Every day, it looks as if the Sun is travelling across the sky. It rises in the east and by midday it's right above your head. Then as evening comes, it sets in the west. But in fact, it's not the Sun that's moving. It's the Earth! As Earth rotates, your part of the world is changing its position in relation to the Sun. This makes it look as if the Sun is moving across the sky.

Earth also moves in another way. It travels around or orbits the Sun. We call the time period that it takes a planet to make one full orbit of the Sun a year.

Earth orbits the Sun once every 365.25 days. A year on Earth is 365 days. But what happens to the other quarter of a day each year? Every fourth year is a leap year with an extra day (29 February) created from the four quarters.

Why Does Earth Have Seasons?

Earth's slight tilt as it orbits the Sun causes our planet to have different seasons. When Earth's northern **hemisphere** is tilted towards the Sun, the north has summer and the southern hemisphere has winter. When the southern hemisphere tilts towards the Sun, the south has summer and the northern hemisphere has winter.

Earth's Seasons

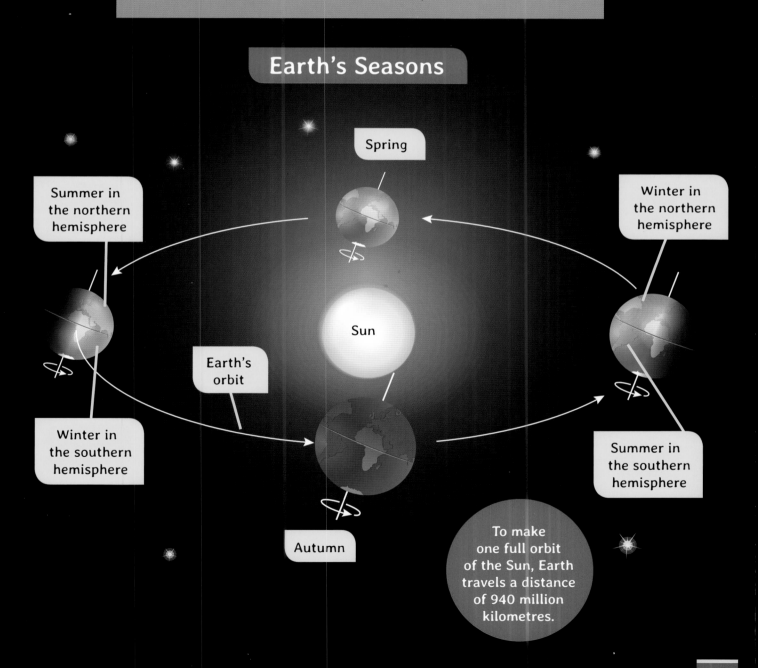

Spring

Summer in the northern hemisphere

Winter in the northern hemisphere

Sun

Earth's orbit

Winter in the southern hemisphere

Summer in the southern hemisphere

Autumn

To make one full orbit of the Sun, Earth travels a distance of 940 million kilometres.

Stonehenge

Ancient people noticed how the Sun changed position in the sky throughout the year. In Britain, skilful **Neolithic** engineers built Stonehenge — a place to celebrate the changing of the seasons.

The remains of Stonehenge stand on a wide open grassland near the modern-day city of Salisbury, in the southwest of England.

Each bluestone weighs about 5 tons.

Bluestones ring

Trilithon

Sarsen stones

Each sarsen stone weighs about 25 tons.

Work on Stonehenge began in about 3100 BC. Workers dug a large circular ditch that measured about 110 metres across. About 500 years later, in around 2600 BC, ancient builders erected a circle of stones, called bluestones, within the ditch.

During the next 200 years, workers added five trilithons (archway-like structures) and an outer ring, all made of enormous sarsen stones.

A Sun Temple

Building Stonehenge took hundreds of people. They had no trucks, heavy-lifting equipment or computers to help them design and build their sun temple. But every giant stone was precisely placed to line up with the rising and setting of the Sun.

Each year, on the morning of the summer solstice (the day with the most hours of daylight), the Sun rises in line with a pathway through the centre of Stonehenge.

On the winter solstice (the day with the fewest hours of daylight), the Sun sets along the same pathway but on the opposite side of the circle.

At midsummer, the Sun rises on this line.

This illustration shows Neolithic people gathering to celebrate the winter solstice.

Shadow cast by stones as the Sun sets

Complete circle of sarsen stones

At midwinter, the Sun sets on this line.

Ditch

The End of Winter

The winter solstice is the shortest day of the year and falls on the 21st or 22nd of December. After this date, the days start to get longer. Ancient people would have celebrated the fact that spring was on the way and it would soon be time to plant crops.

A Midwinter Feast

Near to Stonehenge, **archaeologists** found the remains of a settlement. They found 38,000 bones and teeth buried in rubbish pits, most of which came from pigs.
Tests on the bones show the animals came from Wales, northern England and even Scotland. The tests also showed that the animals were slaughtered in winter.
The bones are good evidence that people came from all over Britain, herding their animals, to enjoy a midwinter feast and celebration at Stonehenge.

The Moon

As Earth orbits the Sun, it is joined by our nearest space neighbour, the Moon.

As they travel through space, the Moon is orbiting Earth. It makes one complete orbit of Earth every 27.3 days.

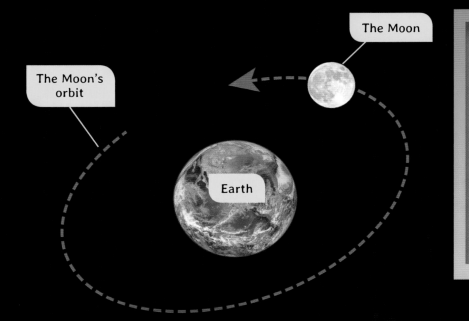

The Moon

The Moon's orbit

Earth

Moon Facts

The Moon looks round but it is actually shaped more like an egg!

The Moon measures 3475 kilometres across.

During the day, temperatures on the Moon reach a scorching 123°C. At night, temperatures drop to −233°C.

Twelve astronauts have walked on the Moon.

The Moon is about 384,000 kilometres from Earth.

Earth

Where Did the Moon Come From?

Many scientists believe that the Moon was created when a large object – perhaps another planet – collided with Earth about 4.5 billion years ago. Rock and other materials from Earth and the colliding planet flew into space. Over millions of years, this material fused, or clumped together, to make the Moon.

Planet crashing into Earth

Unlike Earth, the Moon does not have an atmosphere. When asteroids and other space rocks head for the Moon, they do not burn up in a protective atmosphere. Instead they crash onto its surface, creating hundreds of thousands of **craters**.

Smooth plains

Mountains

Craters

The biggest crater is called the South Pole-Aitken basin. It is 2600 kilometres wide and 13 kilometres deep.

All the impacts from space objects have smashed and broken up the top layer of the Moon's crust. Its surface is covered with dust and rocks – some as big as trucks. This rocky, dusty mixture is called regolith.

Mind-Boggling Space Stuff

Like Earth, the Moon is rotating. But whereas Earth makes one full spin every 24 hours, it takes the Moon 27.3 days to spin around once. These circles show how the Moon spins anti-clockwise. The red part of the circle is the side that's facing Earth. Because of the way the Moon spins as it orbits Earth, we always see the same side of the Moon from Earth (shown in red).

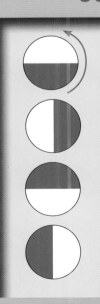

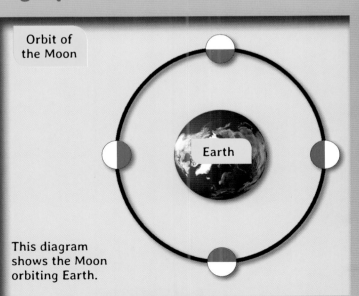

Orbit of the Moon

Earth

This diagram shows the Moon orbiting Earth.

Watching the Moon

When you gaze at the Moon, it sometimes looks as if it is shining with a bright white light. The Moon does not produce light, though. It looks bright because it reflects light from the Sun.

As the Moon makes its orbit around Earth every 27 days, we see different parts of its surface reflecting light. The diagram below shows the phases, or the different looks, of the Moon as it makes one orbit of Earth.

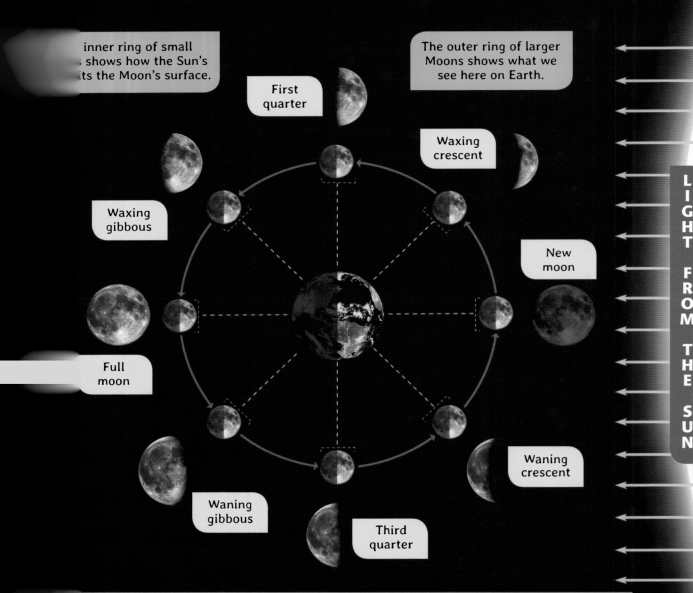

The inner ring of small Moons shows how the Sun's light hits the Moon's surface.

The outer ring of larger Moons shows what we see here on Earth.

First quarter

Waxing crescent

Waxing gibbous

New moon

Full moon

Waning crescent

Waning gibbous

Third quarter

LIGHT FROM THE SUN

Describing the Moon

When the amount of Moon we can see is growing, we say the Moon is waxing. As the Moon seems to get thinner again and starts to disappear, we say it's waning. The gibbous phases get their name because the word *gibbous* means "humped", like the shape of the Moon at these times.

Make a Moon Observation Chart

Discover how the Moon seems to change shape by observing it each night for a month. Often you can see the Moon in the sky even before it gets dark. Download our Moon Observation Chart and get Moon-watching!

Equipment:
• Moon Observation Chart
• Black marker pen

Moon Observation Chart

Name ....

Time to cleck the
Moon each night ....

Date 10th November	Date 11th November	Date 12th November	Date 13th November	Date _____	Date _____	Date _____
Date _____	Date _____	Date _____	Date _____	Date _____	Date _____	Date _____
Date _____	Date _____	Date _____	Date _____	Date _____	Date _____	Date _____
Date _____	Date _____	Date _____	Date _____	Date _____	Date _____	Date _____

Method:

1. Decide what time you will make your observations each night and write it on your chart.

2. At your chosen time, observe the Moon's shape.

3. Fill in the date on your chart. Then colour in that day's section, leaving a white area that matches the shape of the Moon. If it's cloudy and you can't see the Moon, draw clouds for that night's observations.

Make Moon Craters

Equipment:
• Some sand
• Cocoa powder
• A foil baking tray
• Pebbles of different sizes
• A tape measure

Method:

1. Fill the tray with sand and pat it down. Dust some cocoa powder over the top.

2. Take the tray outside.

3. Drop or throw a pebble into the tray. Carefully remove the pebble and it will leave behind a crater.

How far has the rocky regolith (cocoa powder) been ejected from the crater?

Pebble

What can you do to make a deeper crater?

How can you make a wider crater?

4. Keep investigating and make your own crater-covered moon surface.

Let's Talk!

On the Moon, the sky looks black day and night. Why do you think this is?
(The answer is on page 32.)

The Solar System

Were you able to name the eight planets in our solar system? Each one has been orbiting the Sun, on its own pathway around our star for 4.5 billion years.

The eight planets are:

Mercury   Venus   Earth   Mars   Jupiter   Saturn   Uranus   Neptune

This diagram shows how the eight main planets and the dwarf planet Pluto orbit the Sun. The sizes of the planets and their orbits are not true to life.

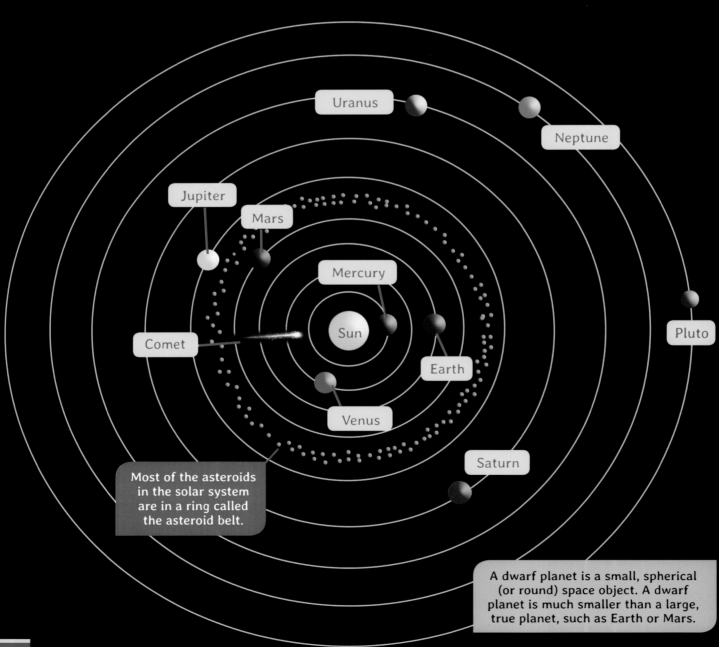

Uranus

Neptune

Jupiter

Mars

Mercury

Sun

Comet

Earth

Venus

Pluto

Saturn

Most of the asteroids in the solar system are in a ring called the asteroid belt.

A dwarf planet is a small, spherical (or round) space object. A dwarf planet is much smaller than a large, true planet, such as Earth or Mars.

The distance between them is not true to life.

Sun

Mercury

Venus

Earth

Mars

Jupiter

Saturn

Uranus

Neptune

All Change for Pluto

Pluto was discovered in 1930 by an astronomer named Clyde W. Tombaugh. For many years, it was called a planet. Then astronomers began discovering other small, planet-like objects orbiting the Sun. They decided to put these objects into their own group and call them dwarf planets. Pluto officially became a dwarf planet in 2007.

Size Comparisons

Earth

The Moon

Pluto

Pluto is a very long way from the Sun. It takes 248 Earth years to make one orbit.

How Long Is a Year?

It takes Earth just over 365 days, or one year, to orbit the Sun. Some planets are closer to the Sun and have a shorter orbit. Mercury's orbit, or year, is just 88 days. Neptune is so far from the Sun that one orbit takes more than 60,190 days. That means a year on Neptune lasts 165 Earth years!

Centre of Attention

It's sometimes possible to see Mercury, Venus, Mars, Jupiter and Saturn without using a telescope. Ancient astronomers knew of these planets and tracked their journeys across the night sky. About 1800 years ago, an astronomer named Claudius Ptolemy put forward a theory that the Sun and planets were orbiting the Earth.

In the 1500s, an astronomer named Nicolaus Copernicus challenged this idea. Copernicus believed that Earth and the other planets were in fact orbiting the Sun. Today we know that Copernicus's theory about the solar system was correct.

The Rocky Planets

Earth and the other three planets that are closest to the Sun are known as the rocky planets. This is because they are made of rock and metal.

Mercury

- Named after the ancient Romans' messenger of the gods.
- 4879 km across
- Length of year: 88 days
- No moons

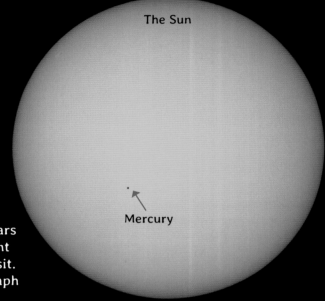

The Sun

Mercury

The Tiny Messenger

Mercury is the smallest of the eight planets. Every few years it can be seen from Earth as a tiny dot as it passes in front of the Sun. This movement across the Sun is called a transit. Astronomers use special equipment to watch and photograph these events so that everyone can safely see them.

Venus

- Named after the Roman goddess of love and beauty.
- 12,104 km across
- Length of year: 225 days
- No moons

This illustration of Venus's surface was created using information sent back by spacecraft that have visited the planet.

The Hot One!

Venus is a rocky, scorching-hot world that is home to more than 1000 volcanoes. Temperatures on its surface reach more than 450°C – eight times hotter than the highest temperature ever recorded on Earth. Some metals would melt on the planet's surface! Venus is surrounded by a thick atmosphere of clouds and poisonous gases. Once heat from the Sun reaches the planet's surface it stays there – trapped by the atmosphere.

Earth

- The word *Earth* is a very old word for "ground".
- 12,742 km across
- Length of year: 365 days
- Earth has one moon

Astronaut Samantha Cristoforetti watches and photographs the Earth from onboard the International Space Station (ISS).

The Living Planet

For now, Earth is the only planet that we know of in the universe where there is life. It is home to microscopic bacteria, enormous blue whales and elephants, birds, fish, billions of insects and spiders and at least 400,000 different kinds of plants. And of course there are humans – intelligent animals that can design and build spacecraft that allow us to travel into space and look back at our own planet.

The Sun

Olympus Mons

Surface of Mars

Mars

- Named after the Roman god of war.
- 6779 km across
- Length of year: 687 days
- Two moons named Deimos and Phobos

A Giant Volcano

Mars is home to the tallest mountain in the solar system – a giant **volcano** named Olympus Mons. It is about 22 kilometres high. That's almost three times the height of Mount Everest, the tallest mountain on Earth. Today, Olympus Mons no longer erupts. The area covered by the volcano is so great that if it were dropped onto Earth, it would almost cover the whole of England!

The Gas Giants

The four outer planets of the solar system are known as the gas giants. It would not be possible to land a spacecraft on these distant worlds because they are made of gases and icy liquids and have no solid surface.

Jupiter

- Named after the king of the Roman gods.
- 139,822 km across
- Length of year: almost 12 Earth years
- Jupiter has at least 79 moons and there are possibly more to be discovered.

The Great Red Spot

Earth compared to Jupiter

The Great Red Spot

Jupiter is the largest planet in the solar system. Fierce storms blow beneath its outer layer of clouds, including a huge hurricane called the Great Red Spot. Astronomers in the 1600s reported seeing a giant spot on Jupiter when telescopes were first invented. If it's the same storm, this means the super-size hurricane may have been blowing for at least 400 years!

Saturn

- Named after the Roman god of farming.
- 116,464 km across
- Length of year: almost 30 Earth years
- Saturn has at least 62 moons and there are possibly more to be discovered.

This artwork shows how Saturn's rings might look up close.

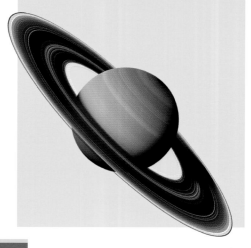

Rings of Rubble

When you look at Saturn through a telescope, it seems to be surrounded by solid, colourful rings. These rings are actually billions of pieces of ice, rock and dust that are orbiting the planet. Some bits of rubble in Saturn's rings are like sand grains and others are house-sized, while a few are the size of mountains!

Uranus

- Named after the Greek god of the sky.
- 50,724 km across
- Length of year: about 84 Earth years
- Uranus has at least 27 moons and there are possibly more to be discovered.

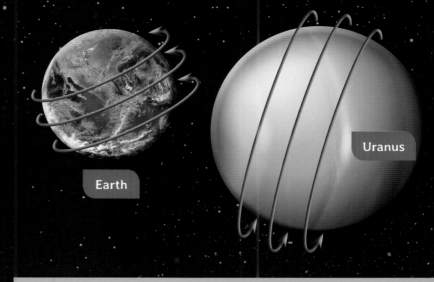

Earth

Uranus

Scientists think the gas giants may each have a solid core made of rock and ice, but at the moment, no one can say for sure.

The Sideways-Spinning Planet

Most planets, including Earth, spin in an anti-clockwise direction. However, Uranus spins clockwise. And instead of spinning in an upright position, this planet spins on its side! Some scientists think that Uranus was hit by another huge space object at some time in its history. The collision would have knocked it from a more upright position onto its side.

This artwork shows how the surface of Triton might look.

Neptune

- Named after the Roman god of the sea.
- 49,244 km across
- Length of year: about 165 Earth years
- Neptune has at least 14 moons and there are possibly more to be discovered.

Frozen

Neptune's largest moon, Triton, is one of the coldest places in the solar system. Beneath its crust of solid ice there are icy liquids. Volcanoes on Triton's surface blast the icy liquid from inside Triton up into the sky. Then the liquid freezes high above the Moon's surface and falls back onto Triton as snow.

The Milky Way

If Earth had a space address, it would be:
Earth,
The Solar System,
The Milky Way,
The Universe

So what is the Milky Way?

This artwork shows the Milky Way as if seen from above.

The centre of the galaxy is a giant ball of millions of stars.

A disc with arm-like curves made of stars.

Our solar system is positioned here.

The Milky Way is a galaxy. It is a huge collection of stars, gas and dust. Our whole solar system is just a tiny, tiny part of the galaxy.

Astronomers estimate that the Milky Way is home to between 200 and 400 billion other stars. Just like our Sun, each of those stars may be surrounded by planets.

Mind-Boggling Space Stuff

How big is the Milky Way? It's big! In 1977, two spacecraft named *Voyager 1* and *Voyager 2* left Earth. Even though they were travelling at almost 55,000 kilometres per hour, it still took them 30 years just to reach the edge of our solar system. The distance across the Milky Way is about the same as 50,000 solar systems laid end to end. When it comes to space, big is truly BIG!

Sometimes our section of the Milky Way can be seen from Earth.

The Milky Way is just one galaxy. Scientists believe there are more than 200 billion galaxies in the universe!

Astronomers and space fans gather for a star party in Texas, USA.

Let's Revise It

Design a Space Game

Think about all the different things you've learned about space and the solar system.

Can you use these facts to design a game that you can play with your friends?

Equipment:
- A large piece of cardboard
- Coloured pens or paints
- Junk craft materials, such as bottle tops, coloured paper, card or paper towel tubes

Method:

1 Think carefully about ideas for a game. Will it have a board? Do you throw a dice? Will you collect cards or objects? Are there questions to answer?

2 Write down your ideas and sketch how your game will look.

3 Now try making the board or other components for your game. Finally, write down the rules and then play!

Was your game fun to play? Was it easy to win?

Can you think of a way to make your game more challenging?

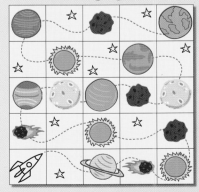

Meet a Space Scientist

Maggie Aderin-Pocock is a space scientist, a **mechanical engineer**, a **communicator** and a woman who has always dreamed of going into space!

"Being a scientist is a fantastic job!"

Maggie Aderin-Pocock

A Clangers toy

Maggie was born in London in 1968. Her first space memory is of loving the TV characters the Clangers and wanting to go into space to live with them.

When Maggie was four years old, her parents split up. Sometimes she lived with her mother and sometimes her father. She moved home a lot and attended 13 different schools.

Regularly changing schools and having **dyslexia** did not hold Maggie back. She developed a passion for science classes, borrowed **physics** books from the local library and became hooked on the TV show *Star Trek*. Her interest and love of space grew and grew. . . .

Maggie worked hard and went to university to study physics and engineering. Since then, she has travelled the world studying space. She has also designed and built pieces of equipment for satellites and telescopes, including the giant James Webb Space Telescope.

Maggie now gives talks about space to schoolchildren and adults around the world. She also presents the BBC's astronomy show *The Sky at Night* — the same TV programme she used to stay up late to watch when she was a little girl!

At just 14 years old, Maggie went to a night school and learned how to make her own telescope!

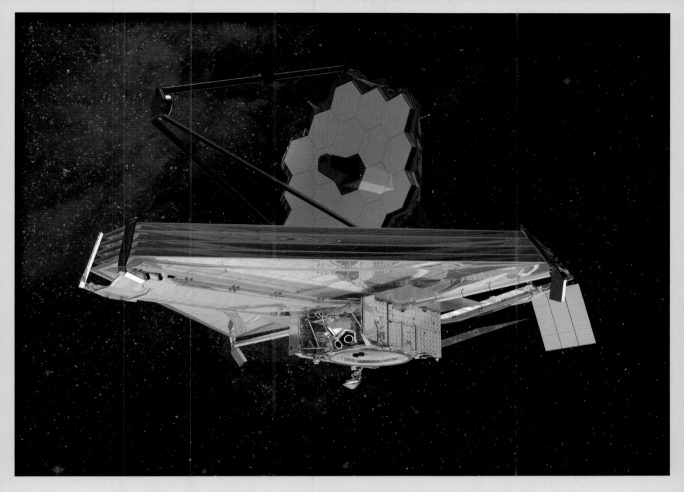

The James Webb Telescope

The mission of the James Webb Space Telescope is to look out across the expanding universe for trillions of kilometres. It will collect images that scientists hope will help them understand how stars, planets and galaxies first formed.

No Boundaries

Maggie was born in Britain and her parents were from Nigeria. Maggie says that sometimes she wasn't sure where she fitted in. In the 1970s, people often didn't accept that someone who was black could be British. Maggie had also never been to Nigeria to get to know that part of her heritage. Maggie says that space seemed to hold the answer:

"When you look at planet Earth from space, there are no countries, there are no boundaries, we're just one people."

Who Can Be a Scientist?

Maggie says that some people are surprised that a black woman became a scientist. She tells everyone that being a scientist is not about gender or your ethnicity. Maggie says:

"What makes a scientist is being inquisitive and wanting to know and understand things. If that sounds like you, being a scientist is the perfect job!"

Glossary

archaeologist
A scientist who studies the past by examining the physical remains left behind, such as bones, monuments and tools.

asteroid
A space rock that's orbiting the Sun. An asteroid can be as small as a car or as big as a mountain.

astronomer
A scientist who studies planets, moons, stars and other natural objects in space. This type of science is called astronomy.

atmosphere
A layer of gases surrounding a planet, moon or star.

comet
A space object made of ice, rock and dust that is orbiting the Sun.

communicator
A person who is good at passing on information — for example, by giving talks or presenting radio or TV shows.

core
The centre of the Earth. It is made of solid metal surrounded by an outer core of molten (super-hot liquid) metal.

cosmologist
A scientist who studies the universe and the beginning (or origins) of the universe.

crater
A large, bowl-shaped hole in the ground, often caused by an impact from an asteroid or other large, rocky space object.

crust
(of the Earth) the outer layer of the planet that is made of rock.

dwarf planet
A spherical object in space that looks like a planet and orbits a star, but is much smaller than a "true" planet.

dyslexia
A learning difficulty that causes a person to face challenges with reading, writing and spelling.

energy
The force that allows things to move and happen. There are different types of energy, such as light energy and heat energy.

evidence
Information that can be used to show that something, such as a theory, is true.

expand
To become larger by spreading outwards.

galaxy
A group of stars, dust, gases and other objects held together in outer space by gravity.

gas
A substance that floats in air and is neither a liquid nor a solid. Most gases, such as oxygen and carbon dioxide, are invisible.

hemisphere
A half of a planet, divided into northern and southern halves by an imaginary line called an equator.

ignite
To start burning and creating heat and light.

mantle
The layer inside Earth between the core and the crust.

matter
Our world and all the real, 3D stuff around us (water, air, metal, rock) is made of what we call "matter".

mechanical engineer
A person who designs, builds or repairs machines.

moon
A space object with a rounded shape that orbits a planet.

nebula
Massive clouds of dust and gases in outer space where stars form.

Neolithic
The last part of the Stone Age. In Britain, this period lasted from about 4500 BC until 2000 BC.

orbit
To circle, or move around, another object.

physics
A science that involves the study of energy, matter and subjects such as forces, light and heat.

planet
A large spherical (ball-shaped) object in space that is orbiting (circling around) a star.

satellite
An object that orbits another object in space. A satellite may be natural, such as a moon, or artificial, such as a satellite used for transmitting TV or mobile phone signals.

solar system
The Sun and all the objects that orbit it, such as planets, their moons, dwarf planets, asteroids and comets.

telescope
An instrument or large machine used for viewing space.

theory
An idea or belief that is based on limited information. A theory can be proved or supported with evidence.

universe
All of the matter and energy that exists and everything in space, including all the planets, stars and galaxies.

Index

Answers

Page 19:
On the Moon, the sky is black whether it is day or night because there is no atmosphere. It's Earth's atmosphere that helps make its sky look blue. Why? Sunlight looks white but it's actually made up of these colours – red, orange, yellow, green, blue, indigo and violet. When sunlight hits Earth's atmosphere, the light gets separated into its different colours and scattered. The blue light gets scattered the most and makes the sky look blue.